D0553628

A GENTLEMAN RAISES HIS GLASS

JOHN BRIDGES

BRYAN CURTIS

Rutledge Hill Press™
Nashville, Tennessee

A Division of Thomas Nelson, Inc.
www.ThomasNelson.com

To Scott Smith,
who never met a glass he couldn't lift

—J.B.

To Perry Uffelman,
who always knows what to say

—B.C.

Published by Rutledge Hill Press, a Division of Thomas Nelson, Inc., P.O. Box 141000, Nashville,
Tennessee 37214.

Library of Congress Cataloging-in-Publication Data

Bridges, John, 1950–
    A gentleman raises his glass / John Bridges, Bryan Curtis.
      p. cm.
    ISBN 1-4016-0110-3 (hardcover)
    1. Toasts. I. Curtis, Bryan. II. Title.
PN6341.B67 2003
808.5'1—dc21   2003004671

Printed in the United States of America
03 04 05 06 07 — 5 4 3 2 1

INTRODUCTION

A gentleman's life is full of happy occasions, some of them formal, some of them as easy-going as a cookout on a Labor Day afternoon. A gentleman knows that on any of these occasions he and his friends may choose to mark the moment by raising a glass, or a bottle, in honor of a special guest or a treasured colleague. The occasion itself may call for a toast for no other reason than to acknowledge the spirit of the moment and the simple pleasure of being among friends. At such times a gentleman should feel most at ease, since he is only being asked to say what is truly in his heart.

It is at just such moments, however, that a gentleman often clinches—particularly if the occasion involves the marriage of his own child, the retirement of a beloved colleague, or his own departure from an organization to which he has given much of himself over a long period. He may also find it difficult to put into words his feelings about the marriage of a long-time friend or the union of two friends whose relationship he has helped nurture.

A gentleman's discomfort may be made greater by the sense that a spotlight is shining in his face. In his heart of hearts, however, a gentleman knows that, if he is the one offering the toast, *he* is not the center of attention. He also knows that he is not expected to wax eloquent or to be quoted in the morning paper. He just says what is in his heart and lets the party proceed.

This book offers some simple guidelines to follow in making toasts, accompanied by some easily adaptable examples. These should not be taken as strict rules that must be followed or as rigid models to be imitated. Rather, they are intended to point the gentleman in the right direction at those times when he chooses to raise his glass and express his respect, admiration, or love for a friend.

A gentleman knows that toasts are intended as tributes and, as such, are a means of celebration.

A gentleman knows that a toast need not be epic in length. Usually a few well-thought-out words are more effective in conveying gratitude or best wishes than an extended tribute would be.

A gentleman knows that the freshest toast of the evening is the first one offered.

To make a toast more personal, a gentleman may elect to include reminiscences and anecdotes. However, he makes sure that the entire assembly, not just the honoree, will appreciate and understand them.

A gentleman knows that, since toasts are intended for celebratory occasions, they require at least moderately formal glassware.

A gentleman knows that, beer steins excepted, he may not toast with anything resembling a coffee cup.

A gentleman does not take it upon himself to deliver a toast at a breakfast meeting.

If a gentleman is asked to deliver a toast at a breakfast meeting, or any meeting before noon, he declines by simply saying, "I'd really prefer not to."

If a gentleman is pressed to deliver a toast at an inappropriate moment, he stands his ground, saying, "No. I'd really prefer you'd ask somebody else to do that. I'm not comfortable making a toast at this time."

A gentleman never uses a toast to ridicule or embarrass a friend. Neither does he use a toast as a sentimental excuse to bring a friend or coworker to tears.

A gentleman knows that he must stand to deliver a toast, except when the event is taking place in a crowded public restaurant.

Even in a crowded public restaurant, a gentleman must at least lean forward toward the others at the table before delivering a toast.

When a gentleman is delivering a
toast to his host or the evening's honoree,
he raises his glass to that person and waits
for other guests at the table to lift their glasses
before he begins his toast. When he has finished
delivering the toast, he may wish to share in
the "clinking" of glasses by touching his
own glass against that of another guest
near him. Once this activity has subsided,
he feels free to take a sip from his own glass.

Before delivering a toast, a gentleman waits until everyone at his table has at least some wine (or some other liquid) in his or her glass.

A gentleman never initiates a toast until the glasses of all the ladies at his table have been filled.

After a toast has been delivered, each guest takes a *sip* from his or her glass.

Knowing that further toasts are likely to follow, a gentleman does not drain his glass after the first tribute has been given.

A gentleman understands that a toast is a public—or at the very least, a semi-public—gesture. He understands that it is most likely inappropriate at a tête-à-tête dinner. If he attempts such a thing, he runs the risk of asking his dinner partner to respond in kind, which boils down to begging for a compliment—pretty much the same thing as asking a friend to say thank you for a thank-you note. Neither of those activities is in any way attractive or socially acceptable.

If a gentleman feels that he must propose a toast at a tête-à-tête dinner, he says nothing more than "Here's to us" or "Here's to our friendship."

A gentleman knows that, when he is asked to make a toast, he does not seize upon the opportunity to do stand-up comedy—even if he is by profession a stand-up comic.

A gentleman does not take it upon himself to deliver the opening toast unless he is the host of the celebration or has been asked to do so by the host or master of ceremonies.

When he is one of a number of scheduled toast-givers, a gentleman does not monopolize the microphone.

If in a series of toasts or tributes, a gentleman hears a story he was going to tell or a toast he was going to make, he does not repeat it. He thinks quickly on his feet and composes a new toast if he is capable of doing so. Otherwise, he makes a simple congratulatory toast, knowing he will have other moments to share his feelings with the honoree.

When a gentleman makes a toast to someone present in the room, he makes it *directly* to that person, not to the table at large.

A gentleman knows that he need not end his toast by saying, "Here's to Tom," "Here's to Gloria," or "Here's to the bride and groom"—although such expressions are never inappropriate. Simply extending his glass toward the honoree is a sufficient conclusion.

A gentleman knows that a toast is not a full-fledged testimonial, outlining the honoree's lifetime achievements and accomplishments.

If possible, a gentleman disdains the use of note cards when delivering a toast. Not only are the cards distracting to him and to his listeners, but they may also require the awkward juggling of glassware and cardstock.

A gentleman knows that even at a bachelor party a toast is intended to be a tribute, not an embarrassment.

In the spirit of fun, a best man may include ribald remarks in his toast at the bachelor party, but at the rehearsal dinner or wedding reception, he keeps it clean, kind-hearted, and concise.

Considering the likely emotional impact of the moment, a father of the bride is especially wise to plan his toast carefully, keeping it brief and, to the best of his abilities, convivial.

A gentleman knows that a well-planned or well-phrased toast should never last longer that sixty seconds.

When making a toast, a gentleman keeps to the point and remembers that he is on the clock.

A gentleman knows that, even in the most celebratory of circumstances, a toast merely underscores the reason for the celebration and is not the celebration itself.

THE TOASTS

A Toast from the Father of the Bride

"Here's to you, Jack. Maddie has been, and always will be, my treasure. I know you will treasure her too. As her father, I have always loved her and always will. Now, as a friend, I pass that same love along to you."

A Gentleman Does Not Say:

"Here's to you, Jack. If you hurt
my little girl, I'll kill you."

A Toast from the
Father of the Groom

"Madeline, even when Jack was a little kid, he had a gift for seeking out the best of everything. I remember when we bought his first catcher's mitt. Joanie and I watched while he tried on every single mitt on the wall at Gillespie's Team Sports, searching until he found just the one he wanted. He chose it not only because it was a beautiful mitt but also because, to his way of thinking, it was the one that fit him best, the one he was going to cherish for a lifetime. He's still got that gift for finding the best of everything, and that's what he's found in you.

"Joanie and I welcome you to our family as if you had always been there. Please know you have all our love."

A Gentleman Does Not Say:

"Madeline, I hope you have
more luck keeping him in
line than I did."

A Toast from the Best Man

"Maddie and Jack, as I watched you exchange your rings during the ceremony, I teared up a little bit. Here was my best friend finally making the commitment to act like a grown-up. But I have to say I was a little envious as well because he was making that commitment to a woman I have come to love and cherish almost as much as if we too had played Little League together.

"I am deeply honored to be a part of this day. I wish you endless days like today, every one of them filled with joy."

A Gentleman Does Not Say:

"Jack, who am I going to
chase hotties with now that you're
off the market?"

A Toast Honoring Lesbian or Gay Friends upon Their Commitment Ceremony

"Rick and Ernie, today is all about two people, each of whom has chosen the other as the person with whom he plans to spend the rest of his life. Each of you is a great guy, loving and generous of spirit, and I am fortunate to call each of you my friend. As you bring all that love and generosity together, who knows what kind of magic will lie before you?

"Thank you for this wonderful day."

A Gentleman Does Not Say:

"It was a beautiful ceremony,
but I live for the day when your marriage
will be considered real."

A Toast Honoring Friends Who Have Been Married Before

"Rachel and Brad, you are people of joy, you are people of wisdom, you are people who know how to value every minute of life. As the two of you come together, joining your families into one great, noisy brood, a whole new family is being formed.

"Thank you for including us in this exciting day."

A Gentleman Does Not Say:

"Rachel, I'm glad you finally came along.
If I'd had to meet one more of Brad's girlfriends,
I would have hung myself."

The Tradition of the Toast

No one really knows how the traditions of toasting and clinking glasses actually began—or for that matter how the word "toast" came to refer to raising a glass in celebration or tribute—but there are a few popular theories.

The ancient Greeks occasionally liked to settle business disputes by dribbling a little poison in the punch. Offering a toast to good health while raising glasses was considered a gesture of good faith, not to mention that there was less risk of being poisoned if all diners were obliged to sip from their own glasses at the same time. Another theory is that the clinking of glasses acted as a deterrent: a victim's tainted beverage could slosh into the glass of the poisoner.

The term "toast" most likely comes from the ancient Romans, who had the habit of putting burnt bread into their wine. Some believe this was to soften the bread, while others say it was to remove the contaminants from impure wine— thus leading to the custom of drinking to one another's health.

A Clink, Not a Crash

A gentleman would never, of course, slam his champagne flute—or his wine goblet, old-fashioned glass, or iced-tea glass—against his partner's glass so smartly as to cause a shattering collision. He simply touches the rim of his glass against the side of the glass most readily offered him. If breakage occurs, he simply asks for a new glass, since the fault clearly is not his own.

A Toast upon a Milestone Anniversary for a Gentleman's Parents

"Mom and Dad, this is a great party, but it still isn't great enough to demonstrate how much we love the two of you. And it could never be fabulous enough to show how grateful we are for all your patience, guidance, and support. You'll notice that I didn't mention your advice since, as you know, most of the time we never took it. But now we know that almost all of the time—except for that time when you wouldn't let me go to Chicago—you were right. In fact, I guess I'd even have to say you were right about Chicago.

"We are one of the luckiest families in existence. I know the two of you are lucky to have each other. But right now, I just want to say how lucky all of us feel to have you.

"Mom and Dad, I love you."

A Gentleman Does Not Say:

"I'm so happy Mom ignored Grandpa's
warning and eloped with Dad. I guess
you showed him."

A Toast upon a Milestone Anniversary
for a Gentleman's Friends

"Linda and Grover, it's an honor for me—and for all of us—to be here as you celebrate forty years of marriage. You are great partners, a great team, and great friends. So many of us have been treated to your generous hospitality over the years, which means that we have had the up-close opportunity to watch you working together and enjoying each other's company. I don't think I've seen either of you actually growl at the other, even when Linda might have needed to say, 'Grover, darling, you know there's *three* days worth of trash in those bags.'

"You've been kind enough to share so many of the good times, and this night is one of those good times. Thank you for including us on this special night."

A Gentleman Does Not Say:

"I know there were times when you were
close to throwing in the towel, but I speak
for everyone here when I say that
I'm glad you didn't."

A Toast upon the Birthday
of a Close Friend

"Olivia, we've come here to celebrate, not just because it's your birthday but also because you are a dear and cherished friend every day.

"Happy birthday, with all our love."

—◄►—

A Gentleman Does Not Say:

"Olivia, you are such a special lady.
I can't believe a man hasn't
snapped you up yet."

A Toast upon a Milestone Birthday of a Gentleman Friend

"Frank, as we raise a glass together to celebrate this monumental day, I can't help but thank my lucky stars, the good Lord above, and your mom and dad for one incredible tennis partner, but more than that—for one incredible best friend.

"Happy birthday, Frank. Here's to many, many more."

A Gentleman Does Not Say:

"Frank, the way you've lived,
who would have thought
you'd make it to fifty?"

A Toast upon a Milestone Birthday of a Lady Friend

"Julie, you make this evening beautiful, just as you make every day of our lives beautiful. It has been my honor to be your friend and to have shared the pleasure of your company through these truly wonderful years. I raise my glass to salute you, for all the good things that you do and for the beauty you bring into the world."

A Gentleman Does Not Say:

"Julie, with the way you look, who would
think you were fifty?"

A Toast Honoring a Friend upon His or Her Graduation

"Babs, it's a special honor to be included in this important moment in your life. All of your friends are fully aware of how hard you've worked. In fact, some of us may even feel that *we're* the ones qualified to go to work as chemical engineers.

"We are so very proud of you, and we all plan to stand back in admiration now as you shoot to the top of your new profession.

"Babs, here's to you."

A Gentleman Does Not Say:

"Babs, one more degree and you will
officially be a professional student—
it's time for you to go to work."

A Toast Celebrating the Baptism, Christening, or Naming of a Child

"What a joyous day this is for Julia and Hugh, but what a happy day it is for the rest of us too. Not only have we witnessed the first celebration in the life of Paige Elizabeth Sims, but we have also been introduced to a new friend, whose life will now be a part of our own.

"We raises our glasses in honor of Paige. May all her days be filled with such brightness and joy."

A Gentleman Does Not Say:

"What I would have given for the
cushy, privileged life this
kid is going to have."

A Toast at a Bar or Bat Mitzvah

"Shelly, I know how hard you've worked to get ready for this important moment. And we are all so proud of you and the splendid job you did in leading this morning's service.

"Your mom and dad were glowing, but so were all of the rest of us who've known you since the day you were born.

"Your joy is our joy on this day. *L'Chaim.*"

A Gentleman Does Not Say:

"Shelly, looks like you hit pay dirt today."

A Gentleman Responds to a Toast

Whenever a toast is proffered in his honor, a gentleman accepts it as the good-intentioned gesture that it is. Although his fraternity brothers or his coworkers may have grown rowdier over the course of the evening, the gentleman resists every urge for one-upmanship. Instead, although everyone else at the table may have stood to toast him and say "Hurrah!" in his honor, a gentleman keeps his seat. When his friends are seated once again, a gentleman stands— immediately, since they may not take another sip from their glasses until he has said his say—and offers the most efficient response possible. He is never wrong to say simply, "Thank you, that was very kind," or at the most, "Thank you, Jim, you're very kind to say those nice words. May I say what an honor and pleasure it is for me to be with you here tonight."

A Gentleman's Friends Join in a Toast

When a gentleman is honored with a toast, his friends wait until the ever-so-brief ceremony is completed and then lift their own glasses to the honoree. They need make no verbal response except to say, "To Larry," "To Mitzi," or "To Mitzi and Mim." A friend is always correct in adding his own hearty "Hear! Hear!"

Next they touch glasses ever so lightly with those persons sitting within convenient arm's reach. No matter how casual the party, once a toast has been offered, a gentleman never rises from his seat to clink glasses with a person at a distant corner of the table. It is helpful to remember that the person at the other end of the table has touched glasses with persons nearer him or her, and this pleasantry has been passed on down the table, glass to glass. A toast, after all, is a communal experience.

A Toast for Mother's Day

"Everybody has a mother, Mom, but you're the one I was lucky enough to be blessed with. And what I was blessed with was selfless devotion, unflinching support, and absolutely unswerving love.

"If other guys can say the same thing about their own mothers, I guess they feel as lucky as I feel today.

"I love you, Mom. Happy Mother's Day."

A Gentleman Does Not Say:

"Mom, I know I'm responsible for the
majority of the wrinkles on your face,
but you're still beautiful to me."

A Toast for Father's Day

"Thank you, Dad, for all the games of catch in the backyard, for all the help with the homework, for the keys to the car, and for that money you wired when I ran out of cash in Paris.

"You really didn't have to do all these things—a lot of guys aren't as lucky as I am. I'm glad you did, though, and today I want to say thank you.

"I love you, Dad. Happy Father's Day."

A Gentleman Does Not Say:

"When I was younger, I thought you
didn't have a clue, but now that
I'm older, I get it."

A Toast for Memorial Day

"I rise now to raise a glass in tribute to all the men and women over the centuries who have taught us to cherish the rights and freedoms with which we are blessed.

"Theirs is the example of devotion, determination, and dedication to which we all should aspire. On this day we honor them for their willingness to make the ultimate sacrifice in order to assure those rights and freedoms for all of us and for all generations to come.

"To those whom we remember by name, and to those whose names we have never heard, let us raise our glasses in humility and thanks."

A Gentleman Does Not Say:

"Here's to a great holiday
and an excuse to drink beer and
go shopping."

A Toast for the Fourth of July

"Let's raise a glass to our country. May we never take for granted the blessings and freedoms that come to us as a birthright. Let us continue to do our best to extend those blessings to men and women everywhere, knowing that freedom is the birthright of all humankind.

"Here's to the United States of America and to a happy Fourth of July."

A Gentleman Does Not Say:

"Here's to the Fourth of July
and a paid day off."

A Toast at Thanksgiving Dinner

"Today, let us count our blessings and not our calories. Happy Thanksgiving to us all."

A Gentleman Does Not Say:

"I'm thankful that my evil ex-wife found
one drop of kindness in her heart and
allowed my kids to join us here today."

A Toast at Christmas Dinner

"This is a season of joy, a season of giving and receiving. There is no greater gift we can give one another than the joy of being together at this time of love and laughter. Simply by being together at this table, the best gift is already unwrapped. We give and we receive.

"Merry Christmas to us all."

A Gentleman Does Not Say:

"Even with the raw turkey, this has
been a pretty good Christmas. Thank
goodness Pizza Hut delivers on holidays."

A Toast for New Year's Eve

"I can't think of a better way to ring in the new year than with a group of people who have been such an important part of my past and, if the heavens are smiling on me, will be an equally important part of my future.

"Here's hoping the new year will bring each of us good health and happiness."

A Gentleman Does Not Say:

"Here's to the new year—it can't be any worse than the last one."

The Gentleman as Toastmaster

From time to time a gentleman may be asked to serve as toastmaster or master of ceremonies on a celebratory occasion. A gentleman feels honored that he has been entrusted to oversee the most festive part of the evening, but he also understands that his job is not one to be taken lightly. He knows that all too easily such an occasion can deteriorate into an "open-mic" night, with every guest expecting to have his or her chance to share memories, either sentimental or sordid.

With the permission of his host or hostess, and well before the night of the party, a gentleman toastmaster plans the sequence of toasts and alerts each toast-giver to his or her place on the agenda. He also suggests to each toast-giver that his or her tribute should last no longer than five minutes.

The Teetotaller at Toasting Time

Many people, for any number of reasons, choose to abstain from drinking alcohol in any form. That decision, however, does not mean they must abstain from the tradition of raising a glass in honor of a good friend, beloved family member, or treasured coworker.

While it is considered bad form—and perhaps even bad luck—to toast with an empty glass, a gentleman feels perfectly comfortable raising a glass half-filled with whatever beverage he chooses. If he chooses to do so, merely in honor of the moment, he may ask that a little wine be poured in his glass so that he may raise his glass and touch it to his lips at the time of the toast. But even that bit of gamesmanship is unnecessary. If a gentleman does not drink alcohol, he feels no pressure to pretend otherwise.

A Housewarming Toast

"Tracey and Gus, as we gather here in this wonderful house, a dream you have worked long and hard to make come true, we wish you a long future of warm winters, flower-filled springs, tree-shaded summers, and red-and-gold autumns. And may this home always be filled with love, peace, and joy for you both, and for all who enter here."

A Gentleman Does Not Say:

"Tracey and Gus, what a great house!
It obviously cost a fortune."

A Toast to Welcome a New
Religious Leader

"Mary Ann, we know that you have been called to us with a sense of mission. We too are called—to be your coworkers, your helpers, and your friends. With you as our rabbi, we know Congregation Emmanuel is headed for even greater service to our community and to the world."

A Gentleman Does Not Say:

"We welcome you, Mary Ann—and as long
as you keep your sermons short, you'll
be with us for a long time."

A Toast upon a Religious Leader's Retirement

"Father O'Reilly, I know you think of us all as your children. You presided at our baptisms, our confirmations, and at so many of our weddings. At all those times, the celebrations were about us. Now the celebration is about you, and like grateful children, we give you our thanks and our love and we say, 'Come back soon, Father.' We know the house isn't going to be the same without you."

A Gentleman Does Not Say:

"Father O'Reilly, we are thankful for all
you have done for us—but most of all
for staying out of the wine cellar."

A Toast to Welcome a New Boss

"Jan, you've bravely chosen to join us. Please know that we intend to support you, realizing that creative ideas and imaginative strategies are the hope of the future. Here's to great days for you and even greater days for Corduroy Concepts."

A Gentleman Does Not Say:

"Jan, we are happy you are here, and if
you last longer than our previous
boss, we'll be even happier."

A Toast upon a Boss's Retirement

"Gary, the past seventeen years have been wonderful for Parity, Inc. Under your leadership the company has grown and flourished and taken the place it so rightly deserves in the Wisterville community. But these have also been wonderful years for me, as you've helped me, like so many others, grow and come to understand my true potential. You are a great leader, but I also consider you a great mentor and a friend.

"You have all my best wishes for many sunlit days on that sailboat of yours. The next time I see you, I expect you to be aglow from the Caribbean sun. Here's to you."

A Gentleman Does Not Say:

"You lucky dog, you are getting out of here
while the rest of us will be sweating it out
every day. I guess that's one good thing
about getting old. Here's to you."

A Toast from a Boss Relinquishing His Position to His Successor

"Jim, I stand here, to pass along to you the great responsibility entrusted to me ten years ago. I have given Gator Graphics my best. I believe you know that your best is what this company deserves. I salute you, knowing that your best is the very best possible. I hope to stand amazed as you lead us on to new heights we have not yet imagined."

A Gentleman Does Not Say:

"Jim, I know you can do this job,
but just in case you find yourself in over
your head, I'm a phone call away."

A Toast from a New Boss in Tribute to His Predecessor

"When Augusta Milbank called me, asking if I'd be interested in coming to Rolofson's, I jumped at the chance, of course. Then, when I realized that she was talking about my possibly succeeding Marvin Gosemark, I said to myself, 'What can you possibly be thinking?' There's nobody in the industry who doesn't have the utmost respect for this man. He is a legend. But I've also learned that he is one of the warmest, most welcoming people I have ever met.

"Thank you, Marvin, for all you've done to make Rolofson's the premier manufacturer of western saddles in the business.

"It's my challenge to maintain his standards. It's my intention to maintain his traditions as well."

A Gentleman Does Not Say:

"I'm going to need everyone's help and
prayers if I'm expected to clean up
this mess I've inherited."

A Toast to Welcome a New Coworker

Marjorie, this is your first day among us. It's a pleasure to have you with us, and we look forward to knowing you and welcoming the fresh energy you bring to Keen Footwear.

"Let me say, 'Welcome,' and I know that everyone here at this moment will join me in saying 'Welcome' too."

A Gentleman Does Not Say:

"I don't know what kind of insanity
you're suffering from that made you come
to work here, but we are glad you did."

A Toast upon a Coworker's Retirement

"Paolo, I still recall the first time we ever met. It was my first day here at the firm, and you were the first person who spoke to me—except maybe for the guy in the elevator, who told me to turn right to find the men's room. I can remember your first words to me: You walked up to my desk, just after I'd taken off my jacket, and said, 'I'm Paolo. We're out of coffee. Come on, I'll show you how to make it so that Gertrude won't yell at you.'

"That's the kind of practical, useful guidance a fellow needs on his first day on the job. And it's the sort of advice, assistance, and guidance you give every day. Your presence hasn't just made this a better firm. It's also made it a better place to work. And it's made the rest of us better folks.

"Paolo, I just want to say thanks for everything."

A Gentleman Does Not Say:

"Paolo, I wish it were me and not you."

A Toast upon the Opening
of a New Business

"Benchley, I know this is a day you've been looking forward to for years now. Now the signs are up and the doors are open.

"What lies ahead is greatness and a nationwide chain of Maple Burger franchises within the next five years.

"Please know how proud we all are of your accomplishments. Congratulations. You deserve every bit of the best."

A Gentleman Does Not Say:

"When times get tough and you're
wondering what in the world made you quit
the law firm and open a burger joint,
your friends are all behind you."

A Toast upon the Happy Closing
of a Business

"For over thirty years now, Frankie, Crosstown Gifts has been a part of all our lives. My parents bought my first teddy bear at your shop, and just last month I bought my new nephew's first teddy bear from you.

"I'm going to miss the chance to simply stop in and browse among all the wonderful items you were able to find, and I'm going to miss the chance to sit down with you late on a Saturday afternoon for one of our impromptu cups of coffee.

"Please know how many good memories you've given all of us. We love you and wish you all the best."

A Gentleman Does Not Say:

"I expect an invitation to that condo in
Boca I helped you buy with all
the money I spent here."

A Toast upon the Not-So-Happy Closing of a Business

"Elbert, we're gathered here tonight to honor you as you stand on the brink of your next adventure. We salute you as a friend, a man of integrity, and a man of vision.

"I am proud to call you my friend. I'm sure everyone here joins me in wishing you great and good things."

A Gentleman Does Not Say:

"I hate those mass merchants. People
will realize what a great store
this was once it's gone."

A TOAST HONORING THE HOST OR HOSTESS AT AN AT-HOME DINNER PARTY

"Sam [or Samantha], thank you so much for this lovely evening. I'd just like to say that you've outdone yourself once again.

"Here's to the heartiness of your hospitality and to this wonderful gathering of friends."

A Gentleman Does Not Say:

"Sam, this was a great party, even with the
burnt bread. It takes a pro to be able
to rise above that."

A Toast Honoring the Host or Hostess of a Restaurant Dinner Party

"Lars (or Lorene), before we get much further into this evening, I'd like to propose a toast to say thank you for this splendid event. It's an honor to be here, among such good friends gathered in this beautiful setting.

"Thank you for making it happen. It's already a night to remember.

"We raise our glasses to you."

A Gentleman Does Not Say:

"Lars, thanks for such a great evening and
for picking up the check."

Toasting in a Restaurant

Many restaurants boast of their care and coddling of "private parties," but a gentleman knows that in a public restaurant no event is ever entirely private, even if it is held in a room completely separate from the main dining area.

Nevertheless, a gentleman knows that dinner in a fine restaurant is an excellent, and generous, way to celebrate a special moment, mark a milestone, or simply treat himself to the company of his most cherished friends. When it comes time for the toasting to begin, and especially if the gentleman's party is seated at a table in the main dining room, both the host and his gentlemanly guests attempt to maintain at least some decorum. The other diners will most likely understand and appreciate the fact that the host's party is a company of devoted friends and relations, but they will *not* appreciate having their own quiet dinners interrupted by a marathon display of toast-giving one-upmanship.

In such a situation, the host and his guests may choose to deliver their toasts without actually rising to their feet, and they make a special effort to resist the temptation to let their toasts wander on as if they were after-dinner speeches. In short, they do their best to keep their intimate celebration as intimate as possible.

Likewise, well-behaved guests at nearby tables feel no urge to invite themselves, or insert themselves, into a celebration intended solely for the gentleman and his guests.

A Toast by a Host, in Tribute to a Friend Who Is Guest of Honor

"Leo, I've asked all these fine folks to join us this evening because I know they all share my love and respect for you. It's as simple as that. To be in your company is plenty of an excuse for a party.

"Permit us all to raise a glass in your honor, as generous soul, great friend, and one of the best golfers on the planet."

A Gentleman Does Not Say:

"Leo, I'm a little drunk, but I'd like to raise a glass to a great friend—my best friend. I love you, man."

A Toast by a Host in Tribute to a Dignitary Who Is Guest of Honor

"My friends, let me ask you to join me now in a toast to our guest of honor, a woman who has paved the way for so many others as a leading light in the field of international diplomacy. In more than thirty years of service to our nation, she has set new standards of integrity, patience, and determination, and her eloquence and composure under fire are the stuff of legend.

"Let us lift our glasses, then, to one of the great women of our generation: Ambassador Evelyn Kalko Early."

A Gentleman Does Not Say:

"I may not agree with your politics,
but I'm honored to be in your presence."

A Toast in Honor of an Out-of-Town Guest

"All of you know that I've asked you to join me this evening so you can meet and share the company of my good friend, Malcolm Zachery. Ever since we met last year at the antique show in Dallas, I've been trying to get him to visit Pondbrook, just so I could introduce him to all of you.

"So I hope you will join me in saying welcome to Malcolm this evening, not just as a friend of mine but as a new friend of yours too. Malcolm, here's to you."

◄►

A Gentleman Does Not Say:

"Malcolm, I'm pleased to introduce you to my friends—and I'm especially glad that they got cleaned up and are on their best behavior.

A TOAST BY A CANDIDATE FOR PUBLIC OFFICE UPON THE COMPLETION OF A SUCCESSFUL CAMPAIGN, IN TRIBUTE TO HIS SUPPORTERS AND STAFF

"Last night was one of the most exciting nights in my life. Standing in front of that microphone, I had the opportunity to say thank you to so many valuable friends and colleagues. I know I mentioned some of you specifically at that time, but it was important to me for us to have this special moment together so that I can tell you how much each of you has meant to me over the past year and a half.

"This has been in every way a team effort. It's my intention to keep the pledges and promises that we have made on the campaign trail. And I know it's going to take teamwork to make that happen too.

"Here's to you, my friends, the heart and soul, the arms and legs, and the smiling face of this campaign."

A Gentleman Does Not Say:

"We showed 'em ."

A Toast by a Candidate for Public Office upon the Completion of an Unsuccessful Campaign, in Tribute to His Supporters and Staff

"Last night was tough for all of us, but late in the evening, back at the hotel, I told Lola that what got me through it was looking out across that ballroom and seeing all of you there, just as you have been there throughout the campaign. There is no better campaign staff anywhere, and a man could have no better friends.

"We got out the message. We did the job.

"I appreciate and cherish the opportunity to have worked with each and every one of you. So here's to you, my friends."

A Gentleman Does Not Say:

"I know that most of you will want to focus
on all the lies my opponent told about me, but we have
to show that we are bigger than he is and move on."

A Toast Congratulating a Candidate upon the Completion of a Successful Campaign

"Roderick, we're here not just to say congratulations but to say thank you for providing the right message at the right time for the people of our community.

"It has been an honor to be a part of this campaign. Please know that all of us appreciate the chance to have been part of this experience, and we all look forward to the great things, and great days, you have in store for our town."

A Gentleman Does Not Say:

"Roderick, now that you've won, we hope
you won't forget all the promises you made
to us. But don't worry, we won't let you."

A Toast in Tribute to a Candidate upon the Completion of an Unsuccessful Campaign

"Roscoe, I know I speak for everyone under this tent, and for thousands of others out there in Metson, when I say thank you for the job you've done over the past eighteen months. Running for office, especially in the way you did it—tirelessly, diligently, and graciously—is in itself a form of public service.

"We are all grateful for the opportunity to have been part of your campaign organization, and we look forward to standing beside you in your next step in life.

"My friends, here's to Roscoe Gaines, still the right man for the job."

A Gentleman Does Not Say:

"Roscoe, I'd like to invite you to have a drink
with me a year from now so we can laugh
at what a mess your opponent has
made of the mayor's office."

A Toast Celebrating an Award or Honor Received by a Friend

"All of us were watching "the Maxxies" last Thursday night, Beryl, when your name was called. There were a lot of happy tears all over town that evening because so many of us know that this award isn't just about your skill as a set designer. It's also about the work you do every day to make the world a better place.

"Nobody deserves this honor more. Please know that we are proud—as we have always been—to be your friends."

A Gentleman Does Not Say:

"Nobody deserves this more, and just think,
I remember when that set you built in high school came
crashing down and you cried like a little girl."

A Toast in Honor of an Outstanding Achievement

"Last year around this time, Roy, nobody knew if Mallory Medical Center was going to make it. Then you stepped up to the plate and said, 'What we need is an effective annual campaign.' And you didn't just say it—you did it.

"Without your determination, your energy, and your refusal to take no for an answer, who knows where the children served by this hospital might be today? Now we know that Mallory will be here for them in the future as well.

"Because you have given them that assurance, we lift our glasses to you."

A Gentleman Does Not Say:

"I don't know if everyone here knows how much your family had to give up so that you could realize this dream, but they should. Here's to your tunnel vision."

A Toast in Recognition of a Heroic or Courageous Act

"Marilyn, we gather here to thank you, not just for your brave deeds, or your alertness in time of trouble, or your willingness to rise to the call of the moment. We also gather here to thank you for reminding us that the human spirit is a wondrous creation. And we thank you for being such a grand embodiment of that spirit."

A Gentleman Does Not Say:

"Marilyn, I didn't think you had it in you."

A TOAST IN MEMORY OF A GREAT FRIEND OR BENEFACTOR

"Everett Elms is with us tonight in many ways: in the presence of his wife and children, in the company of his many friends and admirers, and in the many magnificent gifts he bestowed to worthy causes across our city.

"Let us raise our glasses in his memory, in gratitude for all he taught us and for the example he set. He was a joyful man, and his joy lives on.

"To Everett."

A Gentleman Does Not Say:

"To Everett. I know his wife won't mind
my saying this, but that man could drink
everyone here under the table and still
embarrass us on the tennis court."

A Toast at a Wake or a Funeral Reception

"How splendid it is, I think, to come together here to remember Anthony. Here is the place where he spent so many hours and shared with so many of us the rich and lustrous stories of his life.

"This place will not be the same without him, but it remains enriched by his spirit, his jollity, his goodness, and his concern for his fellow man. All of that is embedded in the walls here.

"To these very walls, then, and to the memory of our dear friend Anthony, let us lift a glass."

A Gentleman Does Not Say:

"Let's lift a glass to Anthony. I'm sure that
if he made it to heaven, he's looking
down on us now and smiling."

When Those Creative Juices Just Aren't Flowing . . .

The following classic toasts are appropriate for those occasions when a gentleman is at a loss for words.

"Here's looking at you." (from *Casablanca*)

"A toast to my best friend, _____, the richest man in town." (from *It's a Wonderful Life*)

"Cheers!"

"All the best."

"To your health."

"'L'Chaim." (Hebrew for "to life")

Did I Really Say That?

Here are a few more simple toasts, ones that might have been considered amusing at some point in time. A gentleman does his best to avoid such tastelessness.

"Live long and prosper."
(from *Star Trek*)

"My advice to you is to start drinking heavily."
(from *Animal House*)

"Here's mud in your eye."

"Here's to good friends. Tonight is kind of special."

"Over the lips, past the gums, look out
stomach, here it comes."

Classic Irish Toasts

No one has mastered the art of the toast like the Irish. Here are a few memorable quotations a gentleman might want to commit to memory for special occasions.

> "May there be a generation of children
> on the children of your children."

> "Here's to health, peace, and prosperity. May the flower of love never be nipped by the frost of disappointment, nor shadow of grief fall among your family and friends."

> "May you be poor in misfortune, rich in blessings, slow to make enemies, and quick to make friends, and may you know nothing but happiness from this day forward."

"May your home always be too
small to hold all your friends."

"We drink to your coffin. May it be built
from the wood of a hundred-year-old oak
tree that I shall plant tomorrow."

"May the good Lord take a liking to
you—but not too soon!"

"There are good ships,
And there are wood ships,
The ships that sail the sea.
But the best ships are friendships,
And may they always be."

"May you be in heaven a full half-hour
before the devil knows you're dead."

"May you live as long as you want and
never want as long as you live."

"May neighbours respect you,
Trouble neglect you,
The angels protect you,
And heaven accept you."

"May the road rise to meet you,
may the wind be always at your back,
the sun shine warm upon your face,
the rain fall soft upon your fields,
and until we meet again may
God hold you in the hollow of his hand."